# TRANSFORM YOUR BODY: FITNESS & HEALTH GUIDE

AF573184

TUSHAR RAJ

Copyright © Tushar Raj
All Rights Reserved.

This book has been self-published with all reasonable efforts taken to make the material error-free by the author. No part of this book shall be used, reproduced in any manner whatsoever without written permission from the author, except in the case of brief quotations embodied in critical articles and reviews.

The Author of this book is solely responsible and liable for its content including but not limited to the views, representations, descriptions, statements, information, opinions and references ["Content"]. The Content of this book shall not constitute or be construed or deemed to reflect the opinion or expression of the Publisher or Editor. Neither the Publisher nor Editor endorse or approve the Content of this book or guarantee the reliability, accuracy or completeness of the Content published herein and do not make any representations or warranties of any kind, express or implied, including but not limited to the implied warranties of merchantability, fitness for a particular purpose. The Publisher and Editor shall not be liable whatsoever for any errors, omissions, whether such errors or omissions result from negligence, accident, or any other cause or claims for loss or damages of any kind, including without limitation, indirect or consequential loss or damage arising out of use, inability to use, or about the reliability, accuracy or sufficiency of the information contained in this book.

Made with ♥ on the Notion Press Platform
www.notionpress.com

This guide is dedicated to anyone who has ever struggled with their fitness and health journey. To those who have felt overwhelmed, discouraged, and defeated, but never gave up on their dream of a healthier and happier life.

To the hardworking individuals who have put in countless hours at the gym and in the kitchen, grinding away to make progress and see results. This guide is a testament to your determination and dedication.

To those who have struggled with mental and emotional health issues, and have learned to channel their struggles into their fitness journey, using it as a form of therapy and a way to heal. Your strength and resilience are inspiring.

And finally, to the friends and family members who have supported us along the way, offering encouragement and love when we needed it most. This guide is dedicated to all of you, and to the hope that it will inspire and empower others on their own fitness and health journey.

# Contents

# Foreword

It is with great pleasure that we introduce you to "Transform Your Body: Fitness & Health Guide." This guide is a comprehensive resource for anyone looking to improve their physical and mental well-being. Whether you are a beginner or have been on a fitness journey for years, this guide will provide you with the knowledge and tools you need to reach your goals.

The focus of this guide is to provide practical and actionable advice on exercise, nutrition, mental and emotional health, sleep, and motivation. Our aim is to help you understand the interplay between these different aspects of wellness and how they can be optimized to support your overall health and well-being.

We have drawn on the latest scientific research and practical expertise to create a guide that is both comprehensive and easy to understand. Whether you are looking to lose weight, build muscle, improve your sleep, or simply feel better, this guide has something for you.

We are confident that the information and advice contained within these pages will be of great value to you as you embark on your fitness and health journey. Whether you are looking to make small changes or undertake a complete transformation, we wish you all the best and know that you will find the guidance and inspiration you need within these pages.

So, what are you waiting for? It's time to take control of your health and transform your body!

# Preface

Welcome to "Transform Your Body: Fitness & Health Guide," a comprehensive guide designed to help you achieve your fitness and health goals. This guide was created to provide you with all the information you need to start your journey to a healthier and happier life.

In this guide, you will learn about the importance of exercise and physical activity, nutrition and diet, mental and emotional health, sleep and rest, and how to stay motivated and track your progress. We will explore each of these topics in depth, giving you the knowledge and tools you need to make positive changes to your lifestyle.

Whether you are just starting out on your fitness journey or you have been working on improving your health for some time, this guide is for you. Whether you want to lose weight, build muscle, improve your overall health, or simply feel better, this guide will provide you with the information and guidance you need to achieve your goals.

Our goal with this guide is to provide you with a comprehensive and easy-to-follow roadmap to transform your body and improve your health. We hope that you find this guide helpful and informative and that it inspires you to take control of your fitness and health journey.

So, let's get started!

# Acknowledgements

This guide would not have been possible without the help and support of several individuals who have been instrumental in its creation.

First and foremost, I would like to express my gratitude to the entire TR GROUP team for providing the platform and resources to write this guide. Their support and encouragement throughout the project have been invaluable.

I would also like to thank my colleagues and friends who have contributed to the guide through their knowledge and expertise in the fields of fitness and health. Their insights and advice have been incredibly helpful in shaping the content of this guide.

I would also like to acknowledge the countless authors, researchers, and health professionals who have provided inspiration and information for this guide. Their work has been a source of guidance and has helped to deepen my understanding of the topic.

Lastly, I would like to thank all of the individuals who have shared their personal experiences and journeys with fitness and health. Their stories have provided motivation and a deeper appreciation for the importance of taking care of our bodies.

I am deeply grateful to all of these individuals and I hope that this guide will be a helpful resource for anyone looking to improve their fitness and health.

# Prologue

Welcome to "Transform Your Body: Fitness & Health Guide"! This guide is designed to help you achieve optimal fitness and health, and live a happier, more fulfilling life. Whether you're a beginner just starting out on your fitness journey, or an experienced fitness enthusiast looking to take your training to the next level, this guide has something for you.

The purpose of this guide is to provide you with the information, tools, and support you need to make lasting changes to your body and health. We will cover a range of topics, including exercise and physical activity, nutrition and diet, mental and emotional health, sleep and rest, and motivation and progress tracking. Our goal is to empower you with the knowledge and resources you need to take control of your body and your health and to help you achieve your goals.

Throughout this guide, you will find helpful tips, practical exercises, and real-world advice from experts in the fields of fitness and health. Whether you're looking to lose weight, build muscle, reduce stress, or simply feel better, this guide is your comprehensive resource for getting fit and feeling great.

So let's get started! Whether you're a seasoned athlete or just starting out, we're confident that you will find the information and support you need in this guide to transform your body and achieve optimal fitness and health.

CHAPTER ONE

# Introduction

Welcome to "Transform Your Body: Fitness & Health Guide"! We're so glad you're here. In this guide, we'll be taking you through all the essential information you need to know about fitness and health. Whether you're just starting your journey or looking to take it to the next level, this guide has something for you.

Purpose of the Guide

The purpose of this guide is to provide you with the information and tools you need to transform your body and achieve optimal fitness and health. We believe that everyone has the potential to be healthy and fit, and we're here to help you get there.

Overview of Fitness and Health

Fitness and health are two sides of the same coin. Fitness refers to your physical ability to perform various activities, while health refers to the overall well-being of your mind, body, and spirit. To truly be healthy and fit, you need to focus on both aspects.

In this guide, we'll cover everything from exercise and physical activity to nutrition, mental and emotional health, sleep, and motivation. We'll provide you with the knowledge and tools you need to make informed decisions about your health, as well as practical tips and strategies for staying on track.

So let's get started! We can't wait to see the amazing transformation you'll make.

CHAPTER TWO

# Exercise and Physical Activity

Exercise and physical activity play a crucial role in achieving and maintaining fitness and health. Regular physical activity can help you improve your cardiovascular health, build muscle strength and endurance, and maintain a healthy weight.

Types of Exercise

There are many different types of exercise, each with its own unique benefits. Some common types of exercise include:

1. Aerobic exercise: This type of exercise gets your heart rate up and improves your cardiovascular health. Examples include running, cycling, and swimming.

2. Strength training: This type of exercise helps build muscle mass and strength. Examples include weightlifting, bodyweight exercises, and resistance bands.

3. Stretching and flexibility: This type of exercise helps improve your flexibility and range of motion. Examples include yoga, Pilates, and foam rolling.

4. Balance and coordination: This type of exercise helps improve your balance and coordination. Examples include tai chi and dance.

Benefits of Regular Physical Activity

* The benefits of regular physical activity are numerous and include:

* Improved cardiovascular health

* Increased muscle strength and endurance

* Better weight management

* Reduced risk of chronic diseases such as heart disease, diabetes, and some cancers

* Improved mental health and reduced stress levels

* Better sleep quality

* Increased energy levels

How to Create a Workout Plan

Creating a workout plan is essential for staying on track and achieving your fitness goals. Here are some tips for creating a successful workout plan:

1. Set realistic goals: What do you want to achieve through exercise and physical activity? Do you want to build muscle, lose weight, or improve your cardiovascular health?

2. Assess your current fitness level: This will help you determine what types of exercise are appropriate for you and set achievable goals.

3. Incorporate a variety of exercises: Mixing up your workouts will help prevent boredom and provide a full-body workout.

4. Schedule your workouts: Make sure to schedule time for exercise in your daily routine. This will help you make it a priority and stick to it.

5. Listen to your body: If you're feeling tired or in pain, it's okay to take a break or modify your workout.

By incorporating these tips into your workout plan, you'll be on your way to achieving your fitness goals and transforming your body.

CHAPTER THREE

# Nutrition and Diet

Nutrition is a crucial component of overall health and fitness, and what you eat can have a big impact on your body and your ability to reach your goals. In this chapter, we'll explore the basics of healthy nutrition and help you understand what you need to know to fuel your body for optimal performance.

Importance of a Healthy Diet

Eating a balanced and nutritious diet is essential for maintaining good health and reaching your fitness goals. A healthy diet provides your body with the nutrients it needs to function properly and can help prevent chronic diseases such as heart disease, obesity, and type 2 diabetes.

In addition to fueling your body, a healthy diet can also improve your mental clarity, boost your energy levels, and promote better sleep. So if you want to feel your best and perform at your peak, it's important to focus on nutrition.

Understanding Macros and Micros

Macros and micros are terms used to describe the different types of nutrients you need in your diet. Macros are macro-nutrients, which include carbohydrates, proteins, and fats. Micros are micro-nutrients, which include vitamins and minerals.

Carbohydrates are the body's main source of energy and are essential for fueling physical activity. Proteins are necessary for building and repairing muscle, and also play a role in energy production. Fats are also important for energy production, as well as for cell growth and repair.

Vitamins and minerals are important for maintaining overall health and play a variety of roles in the body, from supporting the immune system to facilitating metabolism.

Meal Planning and Preparation

Planning and preparing your meals in advance is one of the best things you can do for your nutrition. This not only helps you stick to a healthy diet, but it can also save you time and money.

When planning your meals, aim to include a variety of foods from all food groups, including fruits and vegetables, whole grains, lean proteins, and healthy fats. You can also consider incorporating plant-based protein sources, such as beans, lentils, and tofu, into your diet.

If you're short on time, consider meal prepping for the week on the weekends, or taking advantage of healthy meal delivery services. There are also plenty of healthy and delicious recipes available online, so you're sure to find something that suits your taste buds.

In conclusion, nutrition is a key component of overall health and fitness, and understanding the basics of healthy eating can help you reach your goals. With a little bit of planning and preparation, you can ensure that you're fueling your body with the nutrients it needs to perform at its best.

CHAPTER FOUR

# Mental and Emotional Health

Just as physical fitness is important for our bodies, mental and emotional health are crucial for our overall well-being. In fact, the two are closely connected, and one can have a significant impact on the other. In this chapter, we'll take a closer look at the connection between mind and body and explore ways to support your mental and emotional health.

Understanding the Connection between Mind and Body

The connection between mind and body is undeniable. For example, when you're feeling anxious or stressed, you may experience physical symptoms such as a rapid heartbeat, sweating, or muscle tension. On the other hand, physical activity can have a positive impact on your mental health, reducing symptoms of anxiety and depression and increasing feelings of happiness and well-being.

Stress Management Techniques

Stress is a natural part of life, but it's important to manage it in order to maintain good mental and emotional health. Here are some effective stress management techniques:

1. Exercise: Physical activity has been shown to be an effective way to manage stress.

2. Meditation and deep breathing: These practices can help you calm your mind and reduce stress levels.

3. Time management: By prioritizing tasks and setting realistic expectations, you can reduce stress and avoid feeling overwhelmed.

4. Social support: Spending time with friends and loved ones can help you feel more connected and reduce stress levels.

Building Positive Habits and Attitudes

In addition to managing stress, it's also important to build positive habits and attitudes. This can help you maintain good mental and emotional health and promote overall well-being. Here are some habits and attitudes to focus on:

1. Gratitude: Practicing gratitude can help you focus on the positive aspects of your life and reduce feelings of stress and negativity.

2. Positive self-talk: Instead of criticizing yourself, try to focus on the positive and speak kindly to yourself.

3. Mindfulness: By being fully present in the moment, you can reduce stress and improve your overall mood.

4. Forgiveness: Letting go of resentment and anger can help you reduce stress and maintain good mental health.

In conclusion, taking care of your mental and emotional health is just as important as taking care of your physical health. By understanding the connection between mind and body, managing stress, and building positive habits and attitudes, you can support your mental and emotional well-being and lead a happy and fulfilling life.

CHAPTER FIVE

# Sleep and Rest

One of the most important aspects of a healthy lifestyle is getting enough quality sleep. Sleep plays a crucial role in our overall well-being and is essential for physical, mental, and emotional recovery. Unfortunately, many people struggle with getting enough sleep or experiencing poor sleep quality, which can lead to a wide range of health problems.

Importance of Quality Sleep

Quality sleep is essential for maintaining good health. During sleep, our bodies have the opportunity to repair and rejuvenate. It helps to reduce inflammation, boost our immune system, and regulate hormones. Additionally, adequate sleep is important for maintaining good mental health, as it can help reduce stress and anxiety, improve mood, and enhance cognitive function.

Tips for Better Sleep Hygiene

1. To ensure that you get the best quality sleep possible, there are several things you can do to improve your sleep hygiene. Some tips include:

2. Maintaining a consistent sleep schedule: Try to go to bed and wake up at the same time every day, even on the weekends.

3. Creating a sleep-conducive environment: Keep your bedroom cool, dark, and quiet, and avoid screens for at least 30 minutes before bedtime.

4. Exercise regularly: Regular physical activity can help improve sleep quality and duration. Just be sure to finish your workout a few hours before bedtime.

5. Avoid stimulants: Caffeine, nicotine, and alcohol can all disrupt sleep. Try to avoid these substances for several hours before bedtime.

When to Seek Help for Sleep Disorders

If you're experiencing chronic sleep problems or sleep disturbances, it's important to seek help from a medical professional. Common sleep disorders include insomnia, sleep apnea, and restless leg syndrome. By seeking help, you can get a proper diagnosis and treatment plan to improve your sleep and overall health.

In conclusion, sleep and rest are essential components of a healthy lifestyle. By focusing on good sleep hygiene and seeking help if needed, you can ensure that you're getting the restful and rejuvenating sleep you need to feel your best.

CHAPTER SIX

# Motivation and Progress Tracking

Staying motivated and on track with your fitness and health journey can be a challenge, but it's a crucial aspect of achieving your goals. In this chapter, we'll explore different strategies for keeping yourself motivated and inspired, as well as ways to track your progress so you can celebrate your successes along the way.

Setting Realistic Goals

Setting realistic and achievable goals is the first step in staying motivated. When you have a clear idea of what you want to accomplish, it's easier to stay focused and motivated. Start by setting short-term and long-term goals, and make sure they are specific, measurable, attainable, relevant, and time-bound (SMART). Write your goals down and place them in a visible location, such as your fridge or bulletin board, to keep them top of mind.

Staying Motivated

Staying motivated is key to achieving your fitness and health goals. Here are some strategies to help you stay motivated:

1. Surround yourself with positive people who support your goals

2. Find a workout partner or join a fitness group
3. Set up a reward system for reaching your milestones
4. Celebrate your successes, no matter how small
5. Stay positive and focus on progress, not perfection
6. Remind yourself why you started this journey

Tracking Progress and Celebrating Successes

Tracking your progress is essential for staying motivated and celebrating your successes. There are many ways to track your progress, including:

1. Keeping a journal or log of your exercise, nutrition, and sleep patterns
2. Taking photos to track changes in your appearance
3. Measuring your weight, body fat percentage, or other physical markers
4. Tracking your PRs (personal records) in your exercises
5. Keeping a gratitude journal to reflect on your progress and accomplishments

When you see the progress you've made, it will give you the boost of confidence and motivation you need to keep going. Celebrate your successes, no matter how small, and use them to fuel your motivation.

In conclusion, staying motivated and tracking your progress is essential for achieving your fitness and health goals. By setting realistic goals, surrounding yourself with positive people, and tracking your progress, you'll be well on your way to transforming your body and achieving optimal fitness and health.

CHAPTER SEVEN

# Conclusion

Congratulations on reaching the end of "Transform Your Body: Fitness & Health Guide"! We hope that you've found the information in this guide helpful and informative and that you're ready to continue your journey toward optimal fitness and health.

Final Thoughts

Transforming your body and achieving optimal fitness and health is a journey, not a destination. It's important to remember that there will be ups and downs along the way, but with the right knowledge, tools, and mindset, you can achieve your goals. Stay focused, stay motivated, and most importantly, have fun!

Continuing Your Fitness and Health Journey

The journey towards fitness and health is an ongoing one. It's important to continue learning and growing and to seek out new challenges and experiences. Here are some ways to continue your journey:

1. Join a fitness class or try a new activity
2. Attend a health and wellness workshop or conference
3. Seek out a mentor or coach for guidance and support
4. Experiment with new recipes and cooking techniques
5. Read books, articles, and blog posts on fitness and health

6. Connect with other people who share your interests and goals

In conclusion, your journey toward fitness and health is a lifelong one, and there's always more to learn and discover. Embrace the journey, stay curious, and never stop pushing yourself to be your best.

# Notes

Printed by Libri Plureos GmbH in Hamburg, Germany